A Note to Parents and Teachers

Kids can imagine, kids can laugh and kids can learn to read with this exciting new series of first readers. Each book in the Kids Can Read series has been especially written, illustrated and designed for beginning readers. Humorous, easy-to-read stories, appealing characters and engaging illustrations make for books that kids will want to read over and over again.

To make selecting a book easy for kids, parents and teachers, the Kids Can Read series offers three levels based on different reading abilities:

Level 1: Kids Can Start to Read

Short stories, simple sentences, easy vocabulary, lots of repetition and visual clues for kids just beginning to read.

Level 2: Kids Can Read with Help

Longer stories, varied sentences, increased vocabulary, some repetition and visual clues for kids who have some reading skills, but may need a little help.

Level 3: Kids Can Read Alone

Longer, more complex stories and sentences, more challenging vocabulary, language play, minimal repetition and visual clues for kids who are reading by themselves.

With the Kids Can Read series, kids can enter a new and exciting world of reading!

DISCOVER
SPACE ROCKS

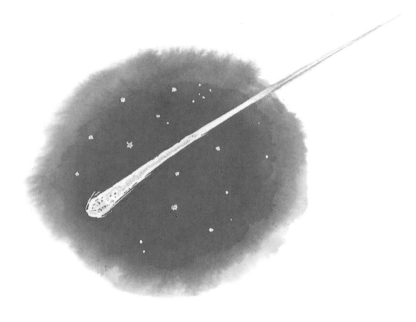

Written by Cynthia Pratt Nicolson
Illustrated by Bill Slavin

Kids Can Press

For their generous sharing of time and expertise, I would like to thank two astronomers: Dr. Tom Gehrels of the University of Arizona and Dr. Colin Scarfe of the University of Victoria. — C.P.N.

Kids Can Read ® Kids Can Read is a registered trademark of Kids Can Press Ltd.

Kids Can Press acknowledges the financial support of the Government of Ontario, through the Ontario Media Development Corporation's Ontario Book Initiative; the Ontario Arts Council; the Canada Council for the Arts; and the Government of Canada, through the BPIDP, for our publishing activity.

Published in Canada by
Kids Can Press Ltd.
29 Birch Avenue
Toronto, ON M4V 1E2

Published in the U.S. by
Kids Can Press Ltd.
2250 Military Road
Tonawanda, NY 14150

www.kidscanpress.com

Adapted by David MacDonald and Cynthia Pratt Nicolson from the book *Comets, Asteroids and Meteorites*.

Edited by Jennifer Stokes
Designed by Sherill Chapman
Educational consultant: Maureen Skinner Weiner, United Synagogue Day School, Willowdale, Ontario

Photo Credits
All photos used courtesy of NASA.

Printed and bound in China

The hardcover edition of this book is smyth sewn casebound.
The paperback edition of this book is limp sewn with a drawn-on cover.

CM 06 0 9 8 7 6 5 4 3 2 1
CM PA 06 0 9 8 7 6 5 4 3 2 1

Library and Archives Canada Cataloguing in Publication

Nicolson, Cynthia Pratt
    Discover space rocks / written by Cynthia Pratt Nicolson ; illustrated by Bill Slavin.

(Kids can read)
Adaptation of the author's Comets, asteroids and meteorites, published 1999 in the series Starting with space.

Age level: Ages 6 to 8.

ISBN-13: 978-1-55337-900-3 (bound). ISBN-10: 1-55337-900-4 (bound).
ISBN-13: 978-1-55337-901-0 (pbk.). ISBN-10: 1-55337-901-2 (pbk.)

1. Comets — Juvenile literature. 2. Asteroids — Juvenile literature.
3. Meteorites — Juvenile literature. I. Slavin, Bill II. Nicolson, Cynthia Pratt. Stars. III. Title. IV. Series: Kids Can read (Toronto, Ont.)

QB721.5.N52 2006   j523.5   C2005-902112-8

Kids Can Press is a *Corus*™ Entertainment company

CONTENTS

Space Rocks 4

Comets 7

Asteroids 17

Meteorites 24

SPACE ROCKS

What happens when rocks drop from the sky? How does a fireball explode in space? Why are comets called dirty snowballs? You are about to find out!

What is a comet?

A comet is an icy, rocky ball that flies through space. Comets circle around the Sun in paths called orbits — just like planets do.

When a comet passes near the Sun, it starts to glow and forms a long tail. Bright comets can be seen from Earth.

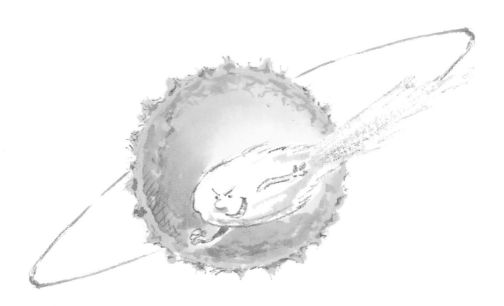

What is an asteroid?

An asteroid is a chunk of rock or metal. Like comets and planets, asteroids also orbit the Sun.

Asteroids are difficult to see from Earth. If you look at an asteroid through a telescope, it looks like a tiny star.

What is a meteorite?

Sometimes asteroids crash into each other. When this happens, small pieces of the asteroids break off. When one of these rocky pieces lands on Earth, it is called a meteorite.

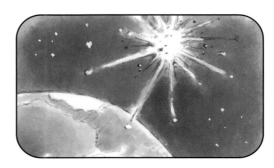

COMETS

A comet looks like a ball of light glowing
in the night sky. Long ago, when people
saw a comet, they didn't know what it was.
Some people were frightened by comets.
They blamed comets for things like storms
earthquakes and diseases.

What are comets made of?

Comets are made of ice and dust. The core of a comet is like a huge, dirty snowball.

When a comet gets near the Sun, a large cloud forms around its core. Wind from the Sun pushes on this cloud to make the comet's long tail. Some comets have more than one tail.

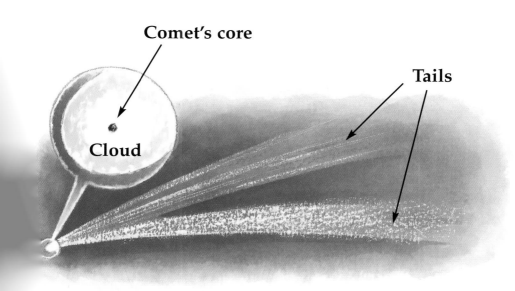

Comet's core

Tails

Cloud

What do comets look like?

Most comets are too small and too far away to be seen from Earth. But when a comet passes near the Sun, its glowing cloud makes it look much bigger and brighter in the night sky.

A bright comet is an amazing sight!

This is Comet Hale-Bopp. Can you see its two tails?

Why do comets seem to stay still?

Things that are far away often look like they're traveling slowly — even when they're really moving fast. Think of an airplane. When you watch from the ground, even the fastest plane seems to move slowly across the sky.

Comets are very far away. That's why they look like they're not moving at all. If you watch a comet over several nights, you'll see that it doesn't stay in the same place.

How long do comets last?

Comets slowly shrink over time. Each time they pass close to the Sun, they lose some of the ice and dust from their core.

Sometimes a comet disappears because it has crashed into a planet or the Sun.

Some comets can last for hundreds or even thousands of years.

This is Comet SOHO 6. It passed too close to the Sun and didn't survive.

How often does a comet appear?

We can see a comet only when it flies close to the Sun. Then it continues on its orbit. We don't see the comet again until the next time it flies close to the Sun.

Some comets have small orbits and appear every few years. Other comets have very large orbits. They appear and then aren't seen again for thousands of years!

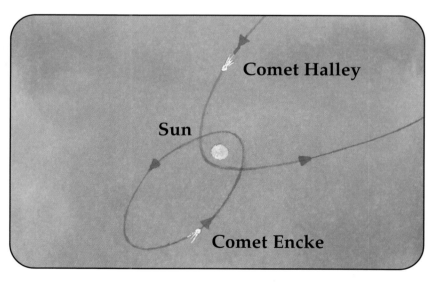

Comet Encke has a small orbit and passes close to the Sun about every three years. Comet Halley has a much larger orbit and passes close to the Sun every 75 years.

How are new comets discovered?

Comet hunters use telescopes to search the night sky. They're looking for a fuzzy spot of light that might be a comet. If they find one, they check a map of all the stars in the sky. They have to make sure that what they saw isn't a star.

When a new comet is discovered, it is named after the one or two people who saw it first.

What happens when a comet hits a planet?

In July 1994, astronomers got to watch a comet crash into the planet Jupiter. Just before the comet hit, it broke into 20 pieces. Some of these pieces made huge explosions when they hit the planet. Other pieces made big dark spots on Jupiter's surface. One of these dark spots was wider than Earth!

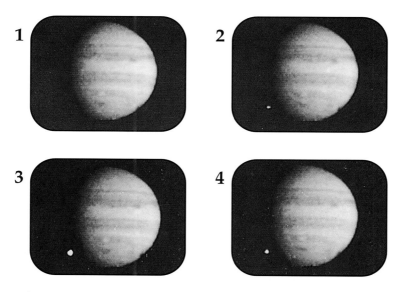

These photos show four pictures of Jupiter. The pictures were taken about two seconds apart. The small white spot in pictures 2, 3 and 4 is a comet crashing into the planet.

Will a comet ever hit Earth?

Comets have hit Earth, but that was long, long ago.

Today, about 500 comets fly across Earth's orbit. Astronomers watch these comets carefully. None of them seem to be headed for Earth.

Comet Facts

• Comet West was last seen in 1976. It was so bright that you could see it in the daytime.

• Caroline Herschel was the first woman to discover a comet. She discovered her first comet in 1786. Then she went on to discover seven more comets!

ASTEROIDS

The word asteroid means "starlike," but asteroids are nothing like stars. They are more like strangely shaped mini-planets.

Most of the time, asteroids just float through space. But, every once in awhile, an asteroid falls to Earth!

This asteroid is 19 km (12 mi.) long!

Did an asteroid kill the dinosaurs?

Some scientists believe that an asteroid may have been the reason dinosaurs disappeared.

About 65 million years ago, when dinosaurs were still alive, a huge asteroid hit Earth. The asteroid exploded when it landed and left a huge hole in the ground. Bits of burning rock flew off in all directions. When the burning rocks landed, they started fires.

Smoke and dust filled the sky, and sunlight could not get through. Plants died because there was no sunlight to help them grow. When the plants died, animals didn't have enough to eat. Soon dinosaurs and many other animals died, too.

Where did asteroids come from?

Our solar system began as a huge swirling cloud filled with dust. The little bits of dust began to stick together and slowly became large rocks. Some of these large rocks smashed together and became planets. The rocky pieces that were left over are what we call asteroids.

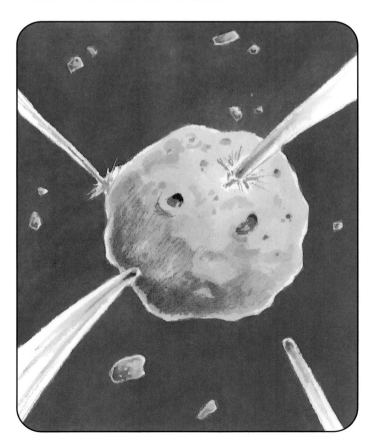

What are asteroids made of?

Most asteroids are made of rock. They are called stony asteroids.

Some asteroids are made of a metal called iron mixed with other kinds of metal. They are called iron asteroids.

A few asteroids are made of both rock and metal. They are called stony-irons.

This photo shows what an asteroid looks like up close.

When was the first asteroid discovered?

Back in the year 1801, a man named Giuseppe Piazzi lived in Italy. One night, he looked through his telescope and saw a tiny object in the sky. It was too small to be a planet. It looked like a small star.

Astronomers decided to call this tiny object an asteroid, which means "starlike." After that, astronomers began to discover more asteroids.

How is an asteroid different from a planet?

Asteroids are much smaller than planets, and asteroids have a different shape than planets.

A planet is round, like a grapefruit. Most asteroids are shaped like lumpy potatoes.

This asteroid has a lumpy shape.

The planet Earth has a round shape.

Asteroid Facts

• The brightest asteroid is named Vesta. If you know just where to look, you can see it with binoculars.

• Small asteroids often come close to Earth. The Moon is very close to Earth, but some of these small asteroids come even closer!

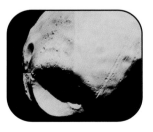

• The planet Mars has two moons. Astronomers think that these moons may really be asteroids.

This is one of the two moons of Mars.

METEORITES

Every day, space rocks travel into the air around Earth. Smaller space rocks burn up and make trails of light in the sky. These trails of light are called meteors.

Larger space rocks crash onto Earth's surface. These are called meteorites.

This hole was made when a meteor as big as a house crashed to Earth. The hole is so big that 20 football fields would fit inside it!

What is the difference between a meteoroid, a meteor and a meteorite?

A meteoroid is a small chunk left behind in space by a comet or asteroid.

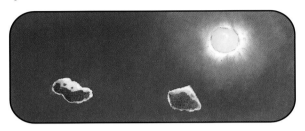

A meteor is the trail of light you see when a meteoroid burns up as it falls to Earth.

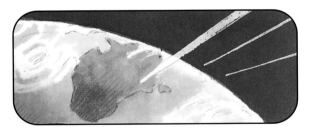

Sometimes not all of a meteoroid burns up as it falls to Earth. The part of the meteoroid that hits the ground is called a meteorite.

Why are meteors so bright?

A small meteoroid travels very quickly. Because the meteoroid is moving so fast, it makes the air around it heat up and begin to glow. When that happens, you see the light of a meteor flash across the sky.

Some of the brightest meteors are made by meteoroids that are no bigger than a grape!

Where do meteorites come from?

Sometimes two asteroids in space will crash into each other. Most meteorites are pieces of asteroids that broke off after a crash.

Meteorites can be made of metal or rock. Some meteorites are made of both metal and rock.

What are meteor showers?

A meteor shower happens when many meteors appear on the same night. We see meteor showers when Earth passes through a trail of dust left behind by a comet.

There are some meteor showers that you can see at the same time every year.

What is a fireball?

A fireball is a very bright meteor. Fireballs are made when a large meteoroid falls toward Earth. Some fireballs are so bright that they can be seen during the day.

Fireballs often make loud bangs or a sound like thunder. Sometimes a fireball explodes in the sky!

In the year 1908, a huge fireball exploded in the sky over Russia. The explosion was so powerful that it knocked down trees over a large area.

What happens when a meteorite hits Earth?

Some meteorites that fall to Earth are so tiny that we don't even notice them. But larger meteorites can cause damage.

We know of only one person who was hit by a meteorite. In the year 1954, Elizabeth Hodges got some bad bruises when a meteorite crashed through the roof of her house.

In 1992, Michelle Knapp heard a crash outside her home. She discovered that her car had been hit by a meteorite the size of a football!

Meteorite Facts

• The largest meteorite in the world fell in Africa. It weighs over 50 tonnes (50 tn.).

• A dog was hit by a meteorite that fell in 1911. Scientists figured out that the meteorite had come all the way from Mars.

• In 1803, thousands of small meteorites rained down on a town in France.

Why do we study space rocks?

Space rocks are amazing. Comets glow when they fly near the Sun. Asteroids smash together in outer space. Meteors flash across the night sky.

Space rocks help us understand how Earth began. They tell us more about our place in the solar system. And they remind us that space isn't empty — it's full of surprises!